# SAYING IT
# WITHOUT WORDS

## Signs and Symbols

# SAYING IT

Books by Arnulf K. Esterer and
Louise A. Esterer
SAYING IT WITHOUT WORDS
    Signs and Symbols
THE OCCULT WORLD

# WITHOUT WORDS

## Signs and Symbols

by Arnulf K. Esterer
and Louise A. Esterer

Julian Messner  New York

Published by Julian Messner, a Simon & Schuster
Division of Gulf & Western Corporation, Simon &
Schuster Building, 1230 Avenue of the Americas,
New York, N.Y. 10020.

Julian Messner and colophon are trademarks
of Simon & Schuster, registered in the U.S. Patent
and Trademark Office.

Manufactured in the United States of America

Design by Philip Jaget

Second Printing, 1982

**Library of Congress Cataloging in Publication Data**

Esterer, Arnulf K
  Saying it without words.

  SUMMARY: Discusses various kinds of signs and symbols
used to convey information quickly and clearly, such as
flags, trademarks, coats of arms, medical symbols,
musical notation, writing, numbers, traffic signs, holiday
symbols, and many others.
  1.  Signs and symbols—Juvenile literature.  [1.  Signs
and symbols]  I.  Esterer, Louise A., joint author.
II.  Title.
AZ108.E79   001.56   79-24287
ISBN 0-671-33037-3

# Acknowledgments

We owe thanks to the following individuals and organizations for their help in various ways in getting material for the book:

Senator Henry M. Jackson, Washington, D.C.
Dr. Eugene D. Farley, Patent Attorney, Portland, OR
Dr. Yuan-Chi Tang, Bellevue, WA
Mrs. Won Liu, Longview, WA
Richard M. Moriarty, M.D., Director, National Poison Center Network, Pittsburgh, PA
Mr. Roy J. Brothers, Ed.D., Superintendent, Washington State School for the Blind, Vancouver, WA
Dr. Fred Knapman, Bellingham, WA
Dr. Henry W. Lennstrom, Dean of Education, Lower Columbia College, Longview, WA
Mr. John C. Page, Director, Editorial Division, Boy Scouts of America, New Brunswick, NJ
Mr. Brooks P. Russell, Director, Crime Prevention Center, Seattle, WA
Ms. Elizabeth Virolainen, British Columbia Provincial Museum, Victoria, BC, Canada
Mr. Robert E. Sconce, Assistant to Grand Secretary, BPOE, Chicago, IL
Mr. Roy Foss, Past Grand Master, Grand Lodge, F&AM of Washington, Spokane, WA
Mr. Jonathan Fiske, Head, Special Procedures, Rotary International, Evanston, IL
Mr. Lloyd W. Ensley, Washington State Highway Department, Olympia, WA
United States Department of Transportation, Federal Highway Administration, Washington, D.C.
Mr. Robert W. DeBuhr, Manager, Longview Chapter, American National Red Cross, Longview, WA
Mrs. Bernelda Roberts, Managing Editor, Forest Products Journal, Madison, WI
Mrs. Ann Williams, Graphics Editor, Forest History Society, Inc., Santa Cruz, CA

Mr. Robert G. Montgomery, Information Manager, Port of Portland,
Portland, OR
Mr. David S. Weedman, Longview, WA
Ms. Lou Ann Paderson, Cowlitz County Emergency Service, Kelso, WA
Staff of the Longview Public Library, Longview, WA
Staff of the Library, Lower Columbia College, Longview, WA
L. S. Nelson, Sheriff, Cowlitz County, State of Washington, Kelso, WA
American Lung Association, New York, NY
Florists' Transworld Delivery System, Southfield, MI
New York Convention and Visitors Bureau, Inc., New York, NY
Saint Louis Regional Commerce and Growth Association, Saint Louis, MO
Blaine Community Chamber of Commerce, Blaine, WA


Thanks are also due to the following companies
for permission to use their logos:


Albertson's Inc., Boise, ID
American Can Company, Greenwich, CO
The Great Atlantic & Pacific Tea Company, Montvale, NJ
Blue Bell Potato Chip Company, Portland, OR
Boise Cascade Corporation, Boise, ID
Bossert Manufacturing Corporation, Utica, NY
Burlington Northern, St. Paul, MN
Eastern Airlines, Miami, FL
Eastman Kodak Company, Rochester, NY
General Foods Corp., White Plains, NY
General Electric Company, Fairfield, CO
General Motors Corp., Detroit, MI
International Harvester, Chicago, IL
Jantzen, Inc., Portland, OR
Japan Air Lines, New York, NY
Kmart Corporation, Troy, MI
Kenwood Corporation, Carson, CA
Loctite Corporation, Newington, CO

3M Company, St. Paul, MN
Nabisco, Inc., East Hanover, NJ
Pacific Northwest Bell, Seattle, WA
Phillips Petroleum Company, Bartlesville, OK
RCA Corporation, New York, NY
Safeco Insurance Company, Seattle, WA
Safeway Stores, Inc., Oakland, CA
Standard Oil Company of California, San Francisco, CA
United Airlines, Elk Grove Township, IL
Varian Associates, Palo Alto, CA
Weyerhaeuser Company, Tacoma, WA
Winnebago Industries, Inc., Forest City, IO
The Wool Bureau, Inc., Woodbury, L.I., NY

# CONTENTS

# Introduction

## *One Look Tells It*

Have you seen signs like these:
 —the arrow on a one-way street?
 —the EXIT sign over doors in the school
 auditorium?
 —the big letter *M* over a hamburger shop
 downtown?

These are a few examples of *signs.* You have
seen many more all around you. A sign tells you
exactly:

—what to do (the arrow tells you which way
   to turn)
—what is there (an exit, a hamburger)
Have you seen:
   —a happy face on your milk mug?
   —the flag of our country waving from a
      building?
   —a drawing of the atom in advertising?

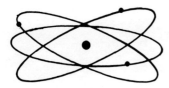

These are a few examples of *symbols*. They tell
*about* something. Symbols are like *pictures of
ideas*.

Look around. See how many signs and symbols
you can find. We use them every day. See how
much they help you to know what to do, or where
to go.

Good signs and symbols tell you something—
and fast! They tell you even if you can't read, or
even if it's in a foreign language.

One look is all you usually need. One look tells
it.

# Chapter 1

## Oh Say, Can You See

Every school day you can see the American flag waving from its pole on the school grounds. Many public buildings as well as homes fly the flag, too, on special days.

You know that our flag is about as old as our country. But did you know that it has five symbols?

The thirteen red and white stripes are symbols for the thirteen colonies which formed the first thirteen states. The stars are symbols of the states—now 50. And the colors are symbols for courage (red), purity (white), and justice (blue).

Why do we have flags? Well, in George Washington's day armies carried flags for identification, to show which side they were fighting on. A field commander had to know whether an approaching army was friend or foe. There was no way then, to send wireless messages as we do today, and a flag could be seen from far away, especially with a telescope. In those days, all ships flew flags for identification, too.

Every one of our states has its own flag. For instance, the New York State flag shows the state coat of arms on a blue background. California shows a grizzly bear on its flag. The grizzly has been wiped out in California, but in 1846, when the state flag was designed, the big and powerful grizzly was a common animal there. The flag of the state of Washington—you could guess it—shows a picture of George Washington on a green background. The green color stands for the Evergreen State. The state flag of Alaska shows the North Star and the Big Dipper, in gold on a blue

New York State

Washington

14

background. These were chosen because Alaska is our northernmost state.

Other countries have their own flags. You can see most of them in front of the United Nations building in New York City. And during the Olympic Games, the flags of all participating nations are paraded at the opening and closing ceremonies. This is a symbol of the unity of all nations in these games. The Olympic Games themselves have their own symbol—five interlocking circles. The rings are colored blue, yellow, black, green and red, in that order. They represent Eurasia (Europe and Asia), Africa, North America, South America and Australia, linked in friendship.

Australia

Just as the colors and symbols in our flag have special meaning for us, so do all foreign flags for the people of their countries. For instance, the flags of Australia and New Zealand show the stars of the Southern Cross on a blue background to indicate that these countries are in the Southern Hemisphere. The Southern Cross can be seen in the sky only in southern countries. It corresponds to the Big Dipper which we see in our northern sky.

New Zealand

15

Israel

People's Republic of China

U.S.S.R.

The flag of Israel shows an old symbol, the 6-pointed Star of David. In ancient times, a star was a symbol of magic. Stars were sometimes worshiped as gods, but the Jewish religion forbade such worship. In later centuries, the religious mystics called a 5-pointed star the Seal of Solomon. Still later, the 6-pointed star was known as the Shield of David. (David and his son, Solomon, were the two greatest kings of ancient Israel.) In the Hebrew language this is Mogen (or Magen) David, which means "Shield of David." As you can see, it is two equal-sided triangles, placed one on the other. The three points of each triangle symbolize God, nature and man. In 1949, this 6-pointed star symbol became officially a part of the flag of the modern state of Israel.

A 5-pointed star is the symbol of communism today. It appears on the flags of the two biggest communist countries, China and the Soviet Union. Their flags are red, which stands for courage and also for blood, and the gold star is the symbol of supreme power. Under the gold star, the Russian flag also shows a crossed hammer and sickle to symbolize the workers in the factories and on the farms.

Many Christian countries use crosses on their

16

flags, because the cross is a symbol of Christianity. Such crosses, for instance, are on the flags of Denmark, Sweden, Finland, Greece and Switzerland. Some countries use an X-shaped cross on their flags. One example is St. Andrew's Cross, the flag of Scotland. It gets its name from St. Andrew, a disciple of Jesus. An old legend says that St. Andrew was crucified on an X-shaped cross.

St. Andrew's Cross

The flag of Britain—the United Kingdom of Great Britain and Northern Ireland—is officially called the Union Jack. It shows the symbols of three countries: England, Scotland and Northern Ireland under one ruler. At first it looks like a puzzle—a criss-cross of red, white and blue. But when you look for the separate parts, you find three crosses, which are symbols of the three countries. England is represented by the thick upright (X shaped) Cross of St. George—red, on a white field. Scotland's symbol is the X-shaped white St. Andrew's Cross on a blue background. There is no symbol for Northern Ireland in the flag. A red St. Patrick's Cross on a white background represents Ireland, which is now an independent nation. But the cross is kept in the Union Jack, since Northern Ireland is historically a part

Cross of St. George

The Union Jack

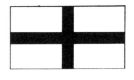

St. Patrick's Cross

17

of the original Ireland. Wales is not separately represented on the Union Jack because it became a part of England many centuries ago.

Another unique flag is that of Japan—a bright red disc on a white field. The red disc is a symbol of the sun, and it can have two meanings. For one thing, it stands for the rising sun. In very ancient times, the Japanese people did not know that the North American continent existed. They believed that their own country, Japan, was the only land that lay in the ocean east of China, and they knew that the sun rose in the east. So they called their own country the "Land of the Rising Sun." And in those days they also believed that their first emperor had been a child of the sun goddess, so the sun on their flag is a symbol of that belief, too.

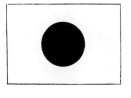

Japan

Flags have been with us for a very long time, probably about 5,000 years. We usually see a flag flying from the top of its staff. The ancient Egyptians considered the staff a symbol of authority. The king carried a short staff—a straight stick with a hook at the top. His subordinates had other staffs. In order to distinguish these staffs from each other, they had different symbols at the tops. Often a piece of colored cloth was tied at the top.

This looked almost like a flag of today.

We still have staffs of authority. You may have seen on TV the Pope or a bishop holding a long staff. Such a staff has a hook at the top and is called a *crozier*. This is a symbol of their authority in the Church, and their work is to be good shepherds. The staff which a bishop carries is a symbol of the good care he takes of his people, in the same way that a shepherd watches over his sheep.

The crozier also looks like the staff which the kings of ancient Egypt carried. Modern monarchs, such as the Queen of England, hold a short, ceremonial stick on occasions of state. This is called a *scepter*.

In the school choir or orchestra, as in all orchestras, the conductor usually holds a short, slim stick. This is a *baton*, the symbol of his or her authority to signal the rhythm and expression to the musicians and singers. Some conductors use their hands only to lead the musicians. But whether hands or baton, the leadership and authority are always there.

Bishop's staff

19

## Chapter 2

# Who Made It?

Maybe you have an alarm clock beside your bed. When the alarm goes off in the morning, you know it's time to get up. The short hour hand, the long minute hand and the fast-moving second hand on the clock are all symbols of time. Most dials on clocks and watches have figures or numerals from 1 to 12, placed in a circle. They stand for the 12 hours of the day or night. The clock's hands and the numerals tell you what time it is.

Clocks were invented after the year 1300. Some had big iron works with wheels inside, which were driven by weights, something like the weights in our pendulum clocks today. Those old clocks were used only in monasteries and public buildings. About 200 years later, the first spring-driven clock was built in Europe. It had a dial with numerals showing the 12 hours, and only an hour hand. So in between the hours, people had to guess what time it was. It was another 150 years after that, before clocks had minute hands and second hands.

Our oldest accurate timepiece is the sun. Around 300 B.C., a Babylonian named Berosus is said to have marked off the sundial into 12 parts, and ever since then we have divided the day into 12 hours. Nowadays we count the 24 hours in a day from 12:00 noon to 12:00 midnight, and from 12:00 midnight to 12:00 noon again. In Biblical times, people counted hours from morning, starting at 6:00 o'clock. So when the Bible says something happened "at the third hour," you can figure it was 9:00 in the morning. "The sixth hour," then, was what we call noon.

You like to have people know who you are, don't you? Well, manufacturing companies and other businesses like that, too. They use trademarks to help the public know who they are. Trademarks are symbols.

Such symbols go way back to the Middle Ages. At that time, skilled craftsmen, working in cities, belonged to unions of their trades. These were called guilds. For example, the goldsmiths had a guild. A goldsmith would punch his symbol on a piece of gold or silverware he had made. It might be his initials. Or perhaps it would be a tiger's head. These figures were first used in England in the year 1300, during the reign of King Edward I. Goldsmiths held their meetings and did official business in Goldsmith's Hall, and the symbols they used were called Hallmarks.

Companies which manufacture goods in this country now use *trademarks*. Like the old-time Hallmarks, trademarks are signs with which a manufacturer marks the products he makes. Trademarks stand for the quality of the product. They are owned by companies, and are registered in the United States Patent Office. When this is done, they legally protect the manufacturer against someone stealing the product's name. Trademarks also protect the buyer and the user against imitations.

*Logo* is another word for the sign that tells you what company made the product. The word *logo* is short for *logogram* or *logotype* (Greek: *logos* = word, written). In modern advertising, this word is often shortened to "logo."

If you get up in the winter at 6:30 in the morning and it's still dark, you can switch on the electric light. It comes mostly from light bulbs, invented in 1879 by Thomas Alva Edison. Today, electric light bulbs are made by several big companies. One is the General Electric Company. You can see their GE trademark on the ends of the bulbs and also on the packages of bulbs you buy at the store.

In the winter, people like to dress in something to keep them warm, maybe wool pants or a skirt, maybe a woolen jacket or sweater. You can tell that clothing is made of 100% virgin wool fiber by the *Woolmark* symbol. This symbol also means that the wool has been used in the garment for the first time.

**PURE WOOL**

The sewn-in Woolmark label is your assurance of quality-tested fabrics made of the world's best...Pure Wool.

And look sharp, because there is another symbol that seems to be the same—the *Woolblend Mark*. Can you see the difference? It means something different, too. The Woolblend Mark on a garment means that the wool in it is blended, or

The Woolmark and Woolblend Mark are certification marks owned by the Wool Bureau, Inc.

The Woolmark and
Woolblend Mark are
certification marks
owned by the Wool
Bureau, Inc.

mixed, with other textile fibers. The other fibers have been added to give greater strength to the fabric, or to help keep it free from wrinkles, or for some other practical reason. Any garment that has the Woolblend Mark must have at least 60% pure wool.

Perhaps something you wear has a trademark showing a beautiful diving girl in a red swimsuit. She is the symbol of Jantzen, Inc., of Portland,

Oregon, manufacturers of fine swimwear and sportswear. This diving girl was first used in Jantzen advertising in 1920, and she has been on the Jantzen swimwear since the mid-1920s. She became so popular that lots of automobile owners, including taxi drivers, pasted her picture onto their windshields.

In *America the Beautiful,* we sing about our "amber waves of grain." Thanks to them, we have a large choice of breakfast foods. All are packaged in boxes or cartons marked with the symbols of their manufacturers. Perhaps you had a Kellogg cereal for breakfast. All Kellogg packages show a copy of Will Keith (W.K.) Kellogg's last name. Mr. Kellogg founded the company in 1906 with Kellogg's Toasted Corn Flakes. He de-

®Used with permission of Kellogg Company.

cided to have his signature printed on every package to make sure customers were buying the best, not an imitation. This symbol of quality and dependability is still printed on every package of Kellogg's cereals and many other Kellogg food products.

Some trademarks are very decorative. One is the Nabisco symbol. The Nabisco name comes from letters in the company name *Na*tional *Bis*cuit *Co*mpany. The symbol is based on an old Italian printing design.

25

After school you may snack on potato chips, so you won't get too hungry before dinner. Some chips are made by the Blue Bell Potato Chip Company. They come in a large box marked by a blue bell, as if it were ringing for dinner time. The blue bell is that company's trademark or symbol or logo.

# BLUE BELL

The Bell Telephone Company also uses a bell as its logo or trademark. This company is an old one, and had the "bell" idea right from its beginning. In those days a bell usually meant a church bell, so the first Bell Telephone logo showed a church bell. That was many years ago, and the bell logo has gone through several changes as you can see below.

If you have a record player, some of your records may be marked with the RCA trademark of the RCA Corporation. The company logo on its RCA records is a little fox terrier with his head on one side, as if he is listening to the music coming from the phonograph horn in front of which he is sitting. The company trademark, "His Master's Voice," is underneath the picture.

Trademarks, RCA and dog-and-phonograph, used with permission of RCA Corporation.

This picture has a true story. One day in Bristol, England, around the year 1890, a painter named Francis Barraud was playing music on his phonograph. Suddenly his black and white terrier, Nipper, jumped up onto the table to investigate. He sat there listening to the sounds coming out of the cone-shaped horn. Barraud painted this interesting picture, and later sold it to the Gramophone Company, Ltd., of London.

In 1900, the trademark, "His Master's Voice,"

was registered with the U.S. Patent Office. The very next year, the Victor Talking Machine Company of Camden, New Jersey, acquired the American rights to the painting, for its trademark.

In 1929, RCA bought the Victor Talking Machine Company, and also the American rights to use the dog-and-phonograph trademark on its records and in advertising and promotional literature.

The story is still going on. RCA has announced a wide new program which uses little Nipper for many company products, on color TV sets, on its service company trucks, on the shipping cartons, and in advertising and promotion.

Do you have a birthday cake on your birthday? If you do, it probably has candles on it, with each candle symbolizing one year of your life. If your mother baked you a chocolate cake, using Baker's Chocolate, maybe you saw on the package the symbol of the Baker Chocolate Company, now a division of General Foods Corp. This picture is of a slim, pretty girl in a long dress and a Dutch cap, holding a tray with a cup on it.

She was a real girl, who lived about 200 years ago. Here is the true story of her picture, *La Belle Chocolatière,* which means The Beautiful Chocolate Girl.

28

The story begins in 1519, when the Spaniards invaded Mexico. They found that the Aztec Indians there made a very tasty drink, *chocolatl*. The Aztecs ground the cocoa bean, beat it to a froth with water, and flavored it with vanilla.

The Spaniards carried the name, the recipe and the ingredients home with them, and slowly the good news spread through Europe. By the year 1700, "Chocolate Houses"—something like our cafes today—were opened in many cities. One day in 1745, in the city of Vienna, Austria, the handsome Prince Ditrichstein stopped in at one of them, to try this fashionable new delicacy. By this time it was being made with milk and sugar, and it was delicious.

The waitress who served the prince that day was a lovely girl, Anna Baltauf. She was poor, but well-born. The prince fell in love with her. He courted her royally, and they were married. For a wedding gift to his wife, he had her portrait painted, life-size, by a famous Swiss artist. In the painting, Anna was dressed as the prince had first seen her—in the cap and full-skirted dress, serving chocolate on a tray.

About 100 years later, the beautiful painting was hanging in the Dresden Art Gallery, and one

day Walter Baker, from Boston, saw it there. Baker was the grandson of the founder of the Baker Chocolate Company. It struck him that *La Belle Chocolatière* would be the perfect trademark for his company's chocolate, and he bought the right to use it for this purpose.

Not all organizations manufacture products, but they still like to have people know who they are. They may use their company symbol or logo on their business stationery and in their advertising. Some logos consist of letters in a pattern, often the initials of a company. Some logos are pictures, some are artistic designs, some try to show how the company's products work. Company logos are registered with the United States Patent Office, and can become trademarks.

A single letter is one of the simplest logos or symbols, and is used by a number of companies. Safeway Stores, Inc., the largest grocery chain in the United States, uses a single red *S* in a circle.

Does your community have an Albertson's grocery store? This big chain has almost 1000 stores. Its logo is a big *A*. Take a close look: the big *A* is

30

more than just a capital letter. The cross-bar is a design of three small leaves, like leaves of growing plants. Albertson's says that these leaves are

planned to give a feeling of growth and dynamic quality. They may also remind you that in one way or another, all the foods we eat come from growing plants.

Do you know the two-letter logo, A & P? This is the symbol of The Great Atlantic & Pacific Tea Company, Inc., another grocery chain, which was founded more than 100 years ago. Old-fashioned letters were in style then, and you may have seen them in old pictures. The old A & P logo used old-fashioned letters. In 1975, the company modernized its logo.

The Great Atlantic & Pacific Tea Company, Inc.

31

Other large organizations also use the letter *A* in their logos. One of these is the American Can Company. This company uses tin, cardboard and

other materials in manufacturing cans, boxes and cartons for packaging. You can see that the artist created this design by bending a flat strip of some material like cardboard or tin.

*K mart* is a large chain of department stores. Its logo shows a big capital letter *K*, with the word *mart,* which means a center for buying and selling. The *K* comes from the name of the parent company, S. S. Kresge, and the logo is the trademark of the K mart Corporation.

K mart is the trademark of the K mart Corporation, and is registered with the U.S. Patent and Trademark Office and in other countries.

The Eastman Kodak Company, in Rochester, New York, manufactures cameras and films. Eastman uses the capital initial *K* in red on a yellow background, with the word *Kodak* also in yellow.

General Motors Corporation is the largest manufacturer of motor cars in the world. Its logo shows two capital letters with a bar underneath: GM. Its largest division is Chevrolet Motor Division, which was named after Louis Chevrolet, a famous Swiss-born racing driver. He designed its first car, and also a later model with which his brother Gaston won two races in Indianapolis. The Chevrolet trademark is called the "bow tie." This design came from wall paper which was seen in a hotel in France.

**General Motors**

Some companies use two or more letters combined in their logos. Look back at the title page of this book, and you'll see one that combines J and M. It stands for Julian Messner, the publisher.

Maybe you've seen two letters combined, in advertisements for 4-wheel-drive cars and pickups, or on heavy-duty trucks. This logo pattern is a small i inside a capital H. It is the symbol of International Harvester, a company which also manufactures farm and construction equipment.

Can you find the *N* in this logo? This is the symbol of the Burlington Northern, the largest railroad company that sends freight cars all over the United States.

**BURLINGTON NORTHERN**

Combinations of initials are sometimes called *monograms* (Greek: *mono* = alone + *gramma* = writing). Some people use their monograms on their stationery. Artists sometimes sign their work with their monograms. A well-known logo of this type was the monogram of Albrecht Dürer, the German painter and engraver. Some of Dürer's best-loved paintings are of a small hare, a violet, and a bunch of flowers. Reproductions of these are still used on greeting cards, and on each one you can see Dürer's famous logo.

The Minnesota Mining & Manufacturing Company could have designed its logo to say MMM. Instead, it used the number 3 and the letter M in the color blue. In 1978, it was redesigned in red.

The most well-known 3M product is Scotch tape. Maybe your family uses it. The various colored tartan patterns on some of the 3M boxes and products remind us of the woolen cloth woven by the old Highland clans in Scotland. Each clan had its own tartan, by which the members were recognized. Today, the tartan patterns of 3M symbolize products that are strong, durable and thrifty, like the Scottish people.

You may find the artistic logos of local businesses in your daily newspaper. They often show you something about the owner's business. The logo of Weedman Garden & Landscaping appeared in The Daily News, of Longview,

Washington. Can you see the W in the tulip? You can probably find interesting logos in your own daily newspaper.

This next logo looks like four capital P's. It is the symbol of the Port of Portland, in Portland, Oregon. It was designed to symbolize the four paths which come together at the port: marine

shipping, aviation, land and people. The port has a big harbor in the Columbia River, and the Portland International Airport. The floors of the air-

port are covered with 240,000 square feet of carpeting, on which the logo shows like a sort of "spider web."

We speak of the transmission of electricity in radio and TV as *waves*. So a wavy line would be a good symbol for companies who manufacture electrical equipment. Varian Associates, in Palo Alto, California, manufactures sophisticated electronic equipment. The company logo is a wave pattern.

Some companies design logos to suggest the kind of work they do. The logo of Bossert Manufacturing Company, in Utica, New York, does this. Bossert makes presses for stamping products out of strips of sheet metal. Can you see how the stamping works?

A logo can be very simple in design, yet give information clearly about the company's products or services. The Loctite Corporation, in Newington, Connecticut, makes strong, close-fitting joints, using threads or adhesives. The Loctite logo tells at a glance that it symbolizes a tight grip.

Here is an S under a roof or shelter. This logo is the symbol of Safeco Insurance Company. Safeco insures clients against loss caused by fire or theft. The roof in the design does seem to offer safety and confidence.

Another sign which offers a good idea of the quality of its products and services is the Chevron sign on service stations. The Chevron company calls its mark a symbol of strength, rank and service, which are its goals. When we see the chevron badge on the uniform sleeve of a United States soldier, we know it stands for the same qualities.

A tree in some form appears in the logos of some very large companies who manufacture wood products, such as lumber, plywood, paper and pulp. The tree symbolizes the raw material which they use in their products. Such logos are often colored green, and you'll see them on trucks, on lumber and sheets of plywood, even on some milk cartons which are manufactured from wood pulp.

A tree symbol in a circle is the logo of Boise Cascade Corporation. Its head office is in Boise, Idaho.

The logo of the Weyerhaeuser Company, based in Tacoma, Washington, suggests two trees, a smaller one inside a larger green triangle, which is also a tree symbol.

**Weyerhaeuser Company**

The Forest History Society, in Santa Cruz, California, has seven triangles in its logo. Doesn't that group of triangles give you an impression of a forest?

 Forest History Society

A tree symbol does not have to mean wood products. A tree can stand for other things, too. Your family's stereo at home may show the name and logo of Kenwood, the manufacturer of stereo equipment. The tree inside the circle stands for "growth," and it means the growth of Kenwood. This company is worldwide. Therefore, the circle in the logo stands for the globe, and Kenwood's message is "Growth Worldwide."

Perhaps you'd like to design a logo for yourself. You might use your own initials. Or you might prefer to plan the design to show something which you like very much, or can do very well—something which you think stands for what you are, or would like to become.

Try it! It would be your own personal symbol.

# Chapter 3

# Taking Care of Your Health

You probably have a medicine cabinet in your bathroom. Do any of the bottles have Mr. Yuk on them? He is a symbol that means *dangerous*. He looks as if the medicine in the bottle doesn't taste good. This symbol was designed at the National Poison Center in Pittsburgh. Dr. Richard W. Moriarty, the director, showed it to some children,

Mr. Yuk, the poison warning symbol of the National Poison Center Network, Children's Hospital of Pittsburgh.

and one little boy said, "He looks yukky!" That's how Mr. Yuk got his name.

Around Mr. Yuk's face is printed a telephone number where you can get help if you accidentally swallow a dangerous medicine. Mr. Yuk is doing a good job, saving children from swallowing medicine that might poison or kill them.

Dangerous medicines have to be taken with the greatest care, and only a doctor can give you a permit for such a medicine. This permit is called a *prescription*. It is usually written on a paper on which is printed the sign $\mathbb{R}$ . This sign stands for the word *recipe*, which means "take" or "use." It tells the pharmacist or druggist what to put into the prescription. Recipe is also the word we use in giving directions for preparing something to eat.

Perhaps you have seen a stubby red cross in a magazine or on a billboard asking for help in time of need, as, for instance, where a disaster has struck. This red cross is an international symbol, and each participating country has its national chapter. In the United States the American Red Cross has offices in most cities.

**the good neighbor.**

The American Red Cross

The Red Cross had its beginning more than 100 years ago. In the year 1859, a young Swiss banker, Jean Henri Dunant, was traveling through northern Italy. Near Solferino, he came to the battlefield where the French and Italian armies had defeated the Austrians, just the day before. More than 40,000 dead and wounded soldiers were lying on the ground. Many of the wounded were struggling to reach the nearest villages for help.

But very little help was available. Mr. Dunant was so upset by the tragic sight of so much suffering, that he set up an emergency hospital in an old church in the nearby town of Castiglione.

Three years later, he told the story of Solferino in a small but very important book. He suggested that permanent, neutral, volunteer organizations be formed in all countries. The next year, sixteen nations sent representatives to Geneva, Switzerland, to organize what we know today as the International Red Cross. Its headquarters are in Switzerland, the country of Jean Henri Dunant. Its emblem is the cross of the Swiss flag, but with the colors transposed. Instead of a white cross on a red background, as in the Swiss flag, the Red Cross flag has a red cross on a white background. The red color of the cross is a symbol of the blood shed in war and in disaster.

Your school may have a chapter of the Junior Red Cross. If it has, perhaps you belong to it.

Maybe you have seen another red cross, this one with two cross-bars. This is the symbol of the American Lung Association. When it was founded in 1904, it adopted the red Cross of Lorraine, as the symbol for the fight against tuberculosis. The original cross was the emblem of Sir Godfrey de Bouillon, the leader of one of the Crusades, more than 750 years ago.

Many barbershops today have a special symbol out in front, a cylinder with a spiral pattern of red and white bands. As the cylinder revolves, the colored bands seem to be disappearing out the top. This symbol of the barbers is several hundred years old.

In those old days, barbers did a lot more than shave customers and cut their hair. They performed minor medical services, such as bandaging wounds and taking care of injuries. Today

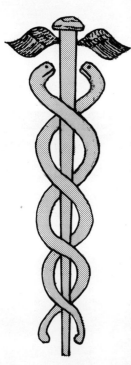

they would be called *paramedics,* meaning that their work is similar in some ways to that of a medical doctor. Those old-time barbers adopted as their professional symbol the white bandage around a bleeding limb. Although this has nothing to do with trimming hair for a customer, the old symbol still stands for the barber.

Does your doctor's office have a picture of a staff with a serpent or snake twined around it? It represents your doctor's "staff of authority," a symbol of his skill in healing. It is called a *caduceus* (ka-doo-se-us), and it is the emblem of the medical profession. You will also see it as part of the insignia of the Army Medical Corps.

The caduceus was the symbol of the ancient Greek god of healing, Asclepius. It was a symbol of authority. But how did the serpent get into the picture?

Well, that story begins in ancient Egypt, about 5,000 years ago. At that time, Egyptian doctors were believed to be the best in the world. They had many recipes for medicines and they performed simple operations.

They had noticed that a snake sheds its skin when it has outgrown it, and grows a new one underneath. You may have seen these discarded snakeskins, yourself, in your own garden, or at

44

summer camp. The Egyptian doctors may have reasoned that if the snake can renew its skin, it might be able to live forever. Therefore, the snake must be a very healthy animal. Thus, the snake became the symbol of good health for human beings.

Much later—about 2,500 years ago—the Greeks borrowed this symbol from the Egyptian doctors. And so the Greek god of medicine is shown with his staff of authority around which winds the serpent as the symbol of health and long life.

# Chapter 4

# Who's Who

Does your mother wear two rings on her left hand? If you asked her about them, she probably told you that the ring with a diamond, or some other gemstone, is called an engagement ring. When your father and mother got engaged, he gave her this ring. The wedding ring is the one he put on her finger during the wedding ceremony. The husband may also wear a plain ring, often the same pattern as his wife's wedding ring.

The third finger of the left hand is called the "ring finger" because in ancient times people believed that a vein ran from this finger to the heart, and it was the heart with which they loved each other. A plain round ring has no end, and this is a symbol of the belief that marriage lasts forever. Most wedding rings are made of gold, because gold is considered a noble metal. Chemicals do not change it, and it cannot be tarnished by perspiration or eggs or onions, or other materials which might touch it in daily life.

Diamonds were set into rings only about 70 years before the American Revolution. At that time, Vincenzo Perussi in Italy learned to grind, or cut, diamonds so they reflect light in brilliant colors. People came to believe that this brilliance is a symbol of the fire of love. A diamond is so hard that it cannot be scratched or harmed by any metal. This hardness and purity of the diamond may have led people to think of it as a symbol of a beautiful and lasting marriage.

About 2,000 years ago, the Romans in Italy wore rings decorated with gemstones, such as rubies, amethysts, emeralds, turquoise, and also pearls. An engaged couple in Rome at that time wore engagement rings on which their names were engraved, as a sign that they belonged to each other. After they were married, the wife wore a wedding ring (sometimes with a key attached) as a symbol of her authority over her household.

It seems that rings were worn even before recorded history. Among the first civilized people were the ancient Sumerians who lived in the Middle East about 5,000 years ago. Sumerian kings and high officials wore rings to show their authority. Such a ring had a flat side, or *table,* engraved with a seal. The official could press this seal into the soft clay on which documents were written, and it served as his sign, or his signature. So these rings were called *signet* rings. The Bible tells us that the king of Egypt placed a signet ring on Joseph's finger, when he made Joseph the overseer of Egypt (Genesis 41:42).

Today many men wear rings with big flat tables. On the table is engraved a large decorative letter, which is the first letter of the person's first or last name.

Sometimes you might see a man wearing a ring with a flat gemstone on which is engraved a special design. This is called a *coat of arms*. The design usually consists of an upper part and a lower one. The lower part represents a shield such as medieval knights in Europe carried. The upper part is called the *crest*. It is a picture or design of the knight's plume-crowned helmet. Such a coat of arms is a family symbol.

Coats of arms started as simple signs which the knights in the Middle Ages wore on their shields for personal identification to tell people who they were. Otherwise, how could you tell whether the knight riding toward you, covered with armor from head to foot, was a friend or a foe?

The coat of arms had to be easily recognized at a distance, so it might have been a vertical or diagonal bar, or a chevron, colored differently from the shield. It might have been a cross. Or the shield might have been divided into halves which were colored differently.

As time went on, coats of arms became quite elaborate. The shield was subdivided into many sections, and each one was decorated with a special pattern or symbol. Symbolic animals might be shown holding up the shield. For example, the coat of arms of the British royal family shows a

lion on one side of the shield, and a unicorn on the other. The lion is a symbol of strength and courage, and the unicorn symbolizes dignity and strength. The unicorn, with one sharp, straight horn on its forehead, does not exist, of course. It comes from the folktales of ancient times.

DIEU ET MON DROIT

Canada was once a colony of Great Britain, and its coat of arms is very similar to the British. However, there is a difference in a section of the shield, and in a flag standing next to it. A stylized picture of a 3-petaled flower is here. This is the *fleur-de-lis,* the French term for lily flower. It is included in the Canadian coat of arms as a reminder that a part of Canada was settled by people who came from France.

According to an ancient legend, an angel gave a fleur-de-lis to Clovis, at his baptism. He was the first French king converted to Christianity, and thereafter he used this flower as his emblem. When kings and nobles were still wearing armor another French king, Charles V, used three of these flowers on his shield, and the fleur-de-lis has been in the French royal coat of arms ever since.

The fleur-de-lis is also the symbol of the Boy Scouts of America, and, with slight changes, of scouts around the world. It is explained as a symbol of peace and purity. Long ago, the mariner's compass used the fleur-de-lis as an ornamental indicator to point straight north. It was adopted as a symbol for scouting to indicate the right way in life.

During the Middle Ages, many lower-class people admired the knights' coats of arms, and they wanted such decorations, too. Some of them had given special services to king and country. Others had given the king large sums of money. In return, the king granted coats of arms to these families or individuals. Later on, even peasants in some countries such as France, wanted such symbols, so that people could see who they were. They often designed their own coats of arms or paid professional artists to design them.

When most countries in Europe became republics, the privileged ruling class, or nobility, was abolished. But people kept on wanting symbols, to help them feel good about themselves, and so coats of arms continued.

In the United States of America, we have no nobility. But the tides of immigration brought into this country many persons and families from Europe. When any of them possessed a coat of arms, they brought it along. Others who wanted to display a family crest tried to find it among relatives or records back in the old country.

When the United States of America was founded, we adopted the eagle as our national symbol. But we were not the first to do so. It was used long ago by the Roman legions, or army divisions. On their standards, or poles, they fastened various signs. At the top would be an eagle which represented the power and swiftness of the legion. After the Roman Empire had crumbled, several of the states that followed adopted the eagle as a symbol in their seals. Today, you can also see it in the seals of Austria, Germany and Poland.

The Great Seal of the United States of America is our official emblem. It was approved in the year 1782 by the Congress of the United States. On it is a picture of the American bald eagle. Across the

eagle's body is a shield, with the red, white and blue of the U.S.A. On one side the eagle's powerful talons hold 13 arrows as a symbol of war (the number 13 stands for the 13 original states). On the other side the eagle holds an olive branch, a symbol of peace. The Great Seal is shown above the doors of all American embassies and consulates throughout the world. It is on all official documents such as treaties. It is also on the uniform buttons of the U.S. Army. And maybe you have noticed it on one side of the Kennedy half-dollar.

Very long ago, people recognized that many animals have superior senses which human beings cannot match. The sharp vision of birds has always impressed man. The ancient Egyptians pictured their sun god, Ra, with the head of a hawk, to show that Ra could see everything!

The Germanic people who lived in Europe about 2,500 years ago also noticed the superior senses of some animals. For example, they knew that the wolf was an excellent runner with a sharp sense of direction. So they chose the wolf as the holy animal of their supreme god, Wotan (or Odin). The wolf symbolized Wotan's power. Children were often named after this animal. One

Anglo-Saxon king was named Ethelwulf, which means "noble wolf." The name Rudolf (in Spanish, Rodolfo) means "red wolf."

When the white settlers came to North America, they found a similar custom among the Indians. Indian names symbolized some of the superior powers of the animals. The name Hawk-eye would suggest eyesight as keen as a hawk's; Sly Fox might mean someone who could be as clever or sly as a fox; Big Bear and Sitting Bull would be names to stand for the size and strength of a bear and a bull. Some Indian tribes even adopted an animal as a symbol for a whole clan. The clans would choose such animals as the panther, the wildcat or the turtle. Then, to show who they were, the clan would place a carving of the chosen animal, or *totem*, on a pole in front of the clan dwelling. Totem comes from the word *ototeman* in the Ojibwa, or Chippewa, language. It means "my family mark."

As time went on, an Indian clan or even a whole tribe would add other totem animals, either through inheritance or through battle conquest over enemies. All such animals were placed to-gether on one pole, one above another. This is what we now call a *totem pole*.

Courtesy of the British Columbia Provincial Museum, Victoria, British Columbia.

The home of the totem pole is among the Indians who live along the Pacific Coast, from the state of Washington up into the Alaska Panhandle. You can see magnificent totem poles in Thunderbird Park, in Victoria, British Columbia. They are carved from red cedar, a wood which is native there. It is soft and easy to carve, and it resists decay for a very long time.

The most famous and widely copied type of totem pole is one on the top of which is a bird with wings outstretched. This is the Thunderbird, an Indian symbol for thunder, lightning and rain. It is actually the American condor, one of the largest

Reproduced with permission of Mrs. Jean Baker Hamilton of Longview, Washington, and Lower Columbia College, Longview, Washington.

flying birds, whose home is in the Rockies and the Andes, where it has great space for gliding or sailing on the updrifts or currents of air. You may have seen the thunderbird symbol on beautiful silver and turquoise Indian jewelry or in men's bolo ties.

The Kwakiutl Indians in British Columbia tell a story about Thunderbird. When their tribe was living in fog and poverty, Thunderbird saw their misery from high above. He pitied them, and came down to earth where he built a fine and comfortable dwelling. Then he invited the Indians to a party. They were amazed at the comfort and beauty of the house, and when they left, they took along everything they could carry. Thunderbird was much upset at this stealing. But what was worse, the Indians took him, too, as their prisoner.

But a violent thunderstorm caught up with them, and they were terrified. Then they noticed that at each lightning flash, their prisoner's eyes blazed, and they realized that he must be their god in human disguise. They begged his forgiveness, and he granted it, on condition that they go home and follow the teachings that he would give them.

# Chapter 5

# Let's Write and Sing

You can read this book because you know the alphabet and how words are spelled. All the letters in our writing and reading are symbols. Each letter stands for a different sound.

This system of writing with letters seems easy. But it didn't come about in an easy way. It took several thousand years and the work of many scholars in ancient foreign lands to develop the alphabet we use today. Without it you couldn't write, you couldn't keep a diary, you couldn't look up information from all over the world and from all the years of our history as human beings. There are many jobs you couldn't hold if you couldn't write and read.

Today, most people in North and South America, in western Europe, in Australia, and in many parts of Africa, use the Latin alphabet of 26 letters. About 250 million other people use the Russian alphabet, which contains Latin, Greek, and some Hebrew letters. Several hundred million others use the Arabic alphabet, and many hundred millions of others use the Hindi alphabet.

But writing symbols for the sounds is not always enough to tell something clearly. We also need some signs to show when an idea ends and a new one begins. For instance, what did actually happen, in this sentence below?

It rained all evening a dog barked behind the tree the moon rose.

This could mean:
It rained. All evening a dog barked behind the tree. The moon rose.
Or it could mean:
It rained all evening. A dog barked. Behind the tree the moon rose.
What would you say it means?

To help us in sorting out meanings in what we write, we use *punctuation,* a system of signs. We put a *period* (.) at the end of a sentence. We use a *comma* (,) when we make a short pause in a sentence. We put a *question mark* (?) or an *exclamation point* (!) at the end of a sentence to indicate a question, or something important. Several other punctuation marks also help us to follow the meaning of the words in a sentence.

But our written alphabet can be used only by people who can see to read and write. In the U.S. alone, there are millions of persons who are blind. Fortunately for them, there is a system which lets them read with the tips of their fingers. This is the Braille alphabet, which is called Braille for short.

Braille was invented in 1824 by a 15-year-old French boy, Louis Braille. When he was three, he had been accidentally blinded by a knife. By the time he was ten, he received a scholarship for the French National Institute for Blind Youth. That was in 1819, when the French army had just developed a system for sending night-time messages, using embossed (raised) dots on a sheet of paper. Young Braille simplified this system, so that a blind person could ''read'' the dots by feeling them with the finger-tips.

The letters in our alphabet, and the numbers from 1 to 9, are represented by only 6 raised dots in various positions.

| 1 | 2 | 3 | 4 | 5 | 6 | 7 | 8 | 9 | 0 |
|---|---|---|---|---|---|---|---|---|---|
| a | b | c | d | e | f | g | h | i | j |

| k | l | m | n | o | p | q | r | s | t |
|---|---|---|---|---|---|---|---|---|---|

| u | v | w | x | y | z |
|---|---|---|---|---|---|

Braille has proved to be a great blessing for millions of blind people all over the world. They are able to read many books and magazines which would otherwise be out of their reach. And in Belgium and Switzerland, banknotes (paper money) are marked in Braille, so that blind persons can still recognize the value of the notes.

Perhaps you know that there are many people

who can see, but cannot hear or speak. They are called *deaf-mutes*. A system to help these people was invented in the 18th century by a French priest, the Abbé Charles Michel de l'Épée, who founded the first school for the deaf in Paris in 1760.

What the Abbé de l'Épée did was to work out an alphabet of hand-signs. Each letter is represented by a position of the fingers and hands. Deaf-mutes learn to use hand signals the same way you learn to speak sounds. Notice how very fast their fingers and hands move in this sign language.

Although our alphabet is useful to us, it may surprise you to learn that more than one-fourth of all the people on earth write with picture symbols, not alphabet letters. Each picture represents a word, and these word-pictures are called *characters*.

Learning to write with word-pictures takes more time than learning to write with the alphabet. But Chinese children can learn to write about 1,500 of these characters between the ages of 6 and 10. This is enough for reading newspapers and short stories.

This system of picture-writing originated in China, about 4,000 years ago. In the beginning, the pictures were made with curved lines. You can still see these pictures in the red seals in the corners of Chinese paintings, or on pieces of very old china. Later on, the Chinese began to write with ink and stiff, pointed brushes, and the lines they drew then became angular.

For example, originally they drew the word *sun* as a circle. But then they reasoned, nothing is perfect in nature. So they placed a dot inside the circle. Drawn with the stiff, pointed brushes, this symbol then turned into ————————→

Sun

The ancient Chinese were also skillful in drawing picture-characters to show action, something in motion, doing something. For example, "to grow" or "to rise" is pictured as a tree rising out of the ground. And when the symbol for *sun* and this tree symbol are drawn together, the character means "sun rising," and they pronounced it *ji-bun*. To the first Europeans who visited China many years ago, this sounded like "Japan," and so that is how they spelled the name of the island nation that lay to the east of China.

All this picture-drawing worked out very well

To rise

Man

Mouth

Word

Honest

when they were drawing pictures of actions or things. But how could you draw a picture of "honest"? Well, the Chinese did it. They drew a man. With his mouth, he speaks words. Now, when a man is combined with his words, this gives the picture-character for "honest," because a man is supposed to speak true words and be honest.

More than 2,000 years after the Chinese had invented their picture-writing, Chinese Buddhist monks traveled to Japan and Korea. In the course of time, they taught the people there the Chinese art of picture-writing. It is still partly in use in these countries today.

Numbers are another kind of useful symbols. For example, the pages of most books have numbers printed on them. With these page numbers you can see at a glance how many pages the book has. And you can find any page you want by turning right to it. You don't have to count all the way through the book till you find the right page.

We call these symbols *numerals*. (Some people call them *figures*.) With numerals you can write down how many people will be coming to your party, or how many dollars and cents you have saved, and so forth.

You can use numerals to do algebra and mathematics. But for this you also need some signs to show you what to do with the symbols. Some of the signs are plus $(+)$, minus $(-)$, times $(\times)$, divided by $(\div)$, equal $(=)$, and so on.

In ancient times, the Romans used numerals in a different way:

| | |
|---|---|
| I = 1 | IX = 9 (1 less than 10) |
| II = 2 | X = 10 |
| III = 3 | XI = 11 (10 + 1) |
| IV = 4 (1 less than 5) | XV = 15 (10 + 5) |
| V = 5 | L = 50 |
| VI = 6 (5 + 1) | C = 100 |
| VII = 7 (5 + 2) | D = 500 |
| VIII = 8 (5 + 3) | M = 1,000 |

You can still see such Roman numerals on old buildings, and in some books to tell the year they were published. For instance, MDCCCLVIII stands for the year 1858. This system does work, but you can see it's clumsy. And it can't be used at all for some figuring. How would you add LXXIV and XXIX? No way! You'd need an abacus with counting-beads.

We owe the numbers we use today to two groups of people—the Hindus in India and the

Arabs. More than 2,000 years ago, the Hindus were using the numerals 1 through 9, as we do now.

About 700 years later, the Arabs in Arabia were developing a new religion, Islam. They believed that Islam was so good, they must carry it far over the earth, to as many people as possible. To do this, they conquered many countries. To the east they reached India, and in the west they invaded Spain. During their contact with the Hindus in India, the Arabs learned to write the numerals the Hindus used. And from Spain, these symbols were slowly adopted by the Europeans, who called them ''Arabic numerals.'' We still call them by that name, today.

In the meantime, people in Europe were developing a great variety of music. Composers wanted to write their music down on paper, so they could keep it for performing and study later. But the 26 letters of the alphabet were not nearly enough symbols for writing music. Music had almost 100 different tones. And besides that, still more signs and symbols were needed to indicate the beat, the time, and many other directions for playing and singing. So the composers of music had to invent them.

If you have been studying music, you have been learning how to use these musical signs and symbols. They are like an ''alphabet'' of music, and players and singers learn to read them just as we read printed words in books and papers. So if playing or singing is something you like to do, you'll be glad that this music ''alphabet'' makes it possible.

# Chapter 6

## Driving Along

Driving along in a car, you can get where you're going faster, stay dry if it's raining or snowing, and bring home packages or other things which would be hard to carry by hand.

There are millions of drivers and pedestrians. To avoid accidents, traffic signs have been installed everywhere—at intersections of city streets, on highways, at crossings for pedestrians or railroads. Drivers have to obey these traffic signs. You have to obey traffic regulations, too, on your bicycle, because the law says that in traffic you are operating a vehicle. All these traffic signs are symbols of safety.

The first traffic sign you notice may be the STOP sign at an intersection. It is a big red octagon with the word STOP. Such a sign is understood in other countries, too. The only difference is the word on the red octagon. For instance, if you drive with your family in Mexico, you'll see a sign that says ALTO. This is Spanish for HALT.

At busy intersections there are traffic lights, either on poles at street corners or hanging up above the center. You know these lights—green for GO, yellow for WAIT, red for STOP. To cross against a red light is a traffic violation. And besides that, it can be very dangerous.

The color *red* was chosen on purpose. It was discovered long ago that in light fog, bright red can still be seen from farther away than any other color. If the fog grows thicker, red is the last color to vanish from sight. This is also why tail lights on motor vehicles are red, and why reflectors on bicycles are red, too. Even if the law does not require red reflectors on bikes, it's a good idea to have one on yours.

The signs that say DON'T WALK for pedestrians are also red for the same reason. There is a section marked on the street for walkers to use

when the sign says WALK or GO. Likewise, there are crosswalks marked on the streets near schools. These may be either white lines or cross-hatched lines.

Downtown you can see still other traffic signs telling what to do. Some are pictures inside red circles, with a slash across the picture, also in red. This type of sign prohibits the driver from doing certain things. Here are some of them.

In some parking areas, you'll see a sign showing a person in a wheelchair. This is for people who cannot walk. No other cars should park in those special places. This is a symbol of kindness, and people who can get around easily should cooperate.

There are other traffic signs to help you be careful. Most of them use the warning symbol of a yellow diamond. On this yellow background are pictures which give the meanings.

Two types of yellow warning signs are not in the diamond shape. A railroad crossing uses a yellow disc with an X and the letters RR. The other yellow sign is shaped like a house, and shows children walking. It warns drivers that a school is ahead.

All of these signs, telling you what to do, and symbols, telling you what something means, give help with instant recognition. You'll find them on interstate, U.S. and state highways and city streets. It's wise to learn about them, even if you're not yet a driver. When you do get your driver's license, you'll be ready.

In addition to all these traffic helps, there are two types of colored signs along the freeways—green guide signs that give directions, and blue service signs.

The blue service signs give information about rest areas, service stations, places where you can eat, telephones, and hospitals. A picture of a telephone tells you there's a place ahead where you can telephone. The hospital sign is a big H with an arrow to show you where to turn off the highway.

The green-background signs give directions for a bike route or a hiking trail. They also provide mileage, route numbers, and exits off the highway.

More than anything else, the people in charge of highway and street safety want traffic to travel at the legal speed limit, or sometimes below it, if a slower speed is safer. Speed signs are posted for this purpose.

But highway supervisors don't leave everything to the drivers. Law enforcement officers in patrol cars watch to see where their help is needed. On interstate highways the state patrol cars show the symbol of their state. On city streets patrol cars are marked with their city symbol. And in the county districts you will find the sheriff in his patrol car with its county symbol. Sheriffs wear their badge or emblem of office—a star with rounded points, and the name of the county. The shoulder-pad emblem of city police is different in each city. Have you noticed the emblem your local policemen wear?

As you drive along, you see the signs and symbols of service stations selling gasoline. Let's look at the symbol of Phillips 66. You notice right away it is in the shape of a shield, and the name is a part of the symbol. But what does the 66 mean?

Well, there's a story behind that. Some people have said that Mr. Frank Phillips was 66 years old when he founded the company. He wasn't—he was 44. Some others have said that Mr. Phillips and his brother had just 66 dollars left when they brought in their first promising oil well. That wasn't true, either.

The true story is even better. It happened in

1927. One of the Phillips company executives was on his way to the meeting at which they were going to choose a trademark for the new gasoline. He remarked to his driver that they were going 60 miles an hour with this gasoline. In 1927, that was fast! "Sixty, nothing!" said the driver. "We're doing sixty-six."

This was great news, and the executive reported it at the meeting. Somebody asked where the car had made such good speed. "It was near Tulsa, on Highway 66," said the executive. That did it! The new gasoline was named Phillips 66.

Other signs you see along the highways are those of motels and restaurants. Many travelers know Howard Johnson's red roof and white spire. Two picturesque names are the Thunderbird and the Red Lion, both operated by the Thunderbird chain. The Thunderbird name makes us remember the Indian story of Thunderbird.

Driving along, you'll see mobile homes going somewhere. Perhaps your family owns one. One very popular type is made by Winnebago Industries, in Forest City, Iowa, and its logo is designed with a large capital *W*. This motorhome

line was named after the county in which the plant and general offices are located. Winnebago is the name of the Indian tribe which once lived in that area.

Any time your family leaves for a trip, you'd like to know that your home is safe while you're away. On many houses you can see a crime prevention symbol next to the front door—the watching eye. It means that family members are watching out for their own safety and property by securing all doors and windows, marking their belongings so they can be recognized if stolen, and their neighbors join them in this. The watching eye watches out for you, and invites you to watch, too. Be a good neighbor!

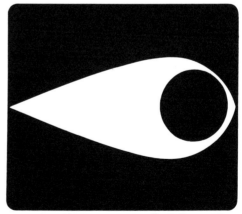

**WARNING**

**OPERATION I.D.**
All items of value on these premises have been marked for ready identification by Law Enforcement Agencies.

# Chapter 7

## Let's Celebrate!

Isn't it fun to have a birthday! Or go to a birthday party! Your birthday is your own symbol of growing up—now you're a year older.

Lots of people have birthday parties, and most of them have cakes with candles. Each candle is a symbol of one year of life. Some people believe that if they blow out all the candles with one breath, any wish they make will come true. Has that happened to you?

Grownups like flowers for celebrating, and they like to send them to friends or relatives, sometimes miles away. But the flowers come, right on time, from a florist in their own town or city. This is due to FTD, the Florists' Transworld Delivery service. You can see the FTD symbol on the card that comes with the flowers. This is a circle with a running man inside it, holding a bunch of flowers. The man is Mercury, the ancient Roman god of commerce and travel. With wings on his shoes and on his helmet, he was the gods' messenger. In the FTD symbol the circle symbolizes the earth, and it means that FTD can deliver fast and everywhere, like Mercury.

The ancient Greeks also had a messenger god, named Hermes. They pictured him with a short staff, called a caduceus, like the one of Asclepius, their god of healing. But the caduceus which Hermes carried had two snakes winding around it, instead of one, and this was a symbol of friendship after a fight. It came about this way: The god Apollo had given Hermes his own staff, made of olive wood, as a reward for a favor. This staff had the mystic power to turn hate into friendship. One day, Hermes saw two snakes fighting on the

ground. He threw down his staff between them, and sure enough the snakes coiled around it and gave each other friendly looks! Hermes then added this image of the friendly snakes to his staff of office.

Valentine's Day comes on February 14. In the Roman Empire, a day of love was also celebrated at the end of winter. Since the heart is the symbol of love, and red is the color of love, cards and gifts were decorated with red hearts. Later, the 14th of February was named after Saint Valentine, who was a martyr in the early Church. So we celebrate our festive day of love on a day named after a saint.

Then comes Easter, a holiday which also has its symbols. Hundreds of years ago, the people who lived in western and northern Europe believed in a spring goddess, Eostre (or Ostara), and they honored her with a spring festival which they called Eostur. Her holy animal was the hare, or rabbit.

In ancient Persia the people believed that the earth had originally come out of a huge egg. In the spring they colored eggs with the colors of spring, and gave them to their friends as symbols of friendship. Nowadays, two of our Easter symbols are colored eggs and rabbits.

78

In summer comes Independence Day. Our American Declaration of Independence was signed on the Fourth of July, and to symbolize the new nation a new flag was created—red, white and blue, the Stars and Stripes. On Independence Day you'll see lots of American flags flying outdoors in the sunshine.

You know what we celebrate on October 31— Trick or Treat! Halloween is a very old festival. More than 2,000 years ago, the Scottish and Irish people believed that fairies, elves, witches and other spirits flew around on that night. The people wanted protection, so they lighted bonfires and placed lighted candles inside hollowed-out turnips.

Today, we don't believe in spirits that fly around playing tricks. But children enjoy dressing up like magic spirits and other interesting characters, and go around visiting their friends and receiving treats. When settlers from the British Isles first came to the New World, they found pumpkins, grown by the American Indians. A pumpkin is bigger than a turnip, so the newcomers took over the pumpkins for their Halloween lanterns. Some people called them Jack o' Lanterns.

A few weeks after Halloween, we enjoy Thanksgiving. And then everybody starts getting ready for either Christmas or Hanukkah, or perhaps both.

Beginning four Sundays before Christmas, many people light the candles of Advent in churches and homes. On the first Sunday, the first candle is lighted, and one more on each of the next three Sundays. The Advent candles symbolize what Jesus said: "I am the light of the world."

During this same time, Jewish families celebrate Hanukkah, the Feast of Lights. Hanukkah continues for eight days. On each day, one candle is lighted on the nine-branched Menorah, with the caretaker candle in the center and four candles at each side.

The eight side candles symbolize the miracle which happened in 165 B.C., after Judas Maccabaeus and the Jewish freedom fighters defeated the Syrian tyrant Antiochus. The freedom fighters regained the sacred temple, which had been defiled, and they relighted the sacred flame in the sanctuary. But there was only enough oil for one day. That was when the miracle occurred! The oil lasted for eight days, until there was time to prepare more sacred oil for the temple.

The ancient Romans also had a winter celebration. In the middle of January, they decorated their homes with laurel and evergreens, to symbolize the cycle of the year's seasons. Even in the winter, when all vegetation seems dead, they knew that plants will grow and be green again. Nowadays, many people hang evergreen boughs or wreaths on their front doors, and decorate Christmas trees.

The custom of lighting a Christmas tree came from Germany, about 400 years ago, where Martin Luther is said to have set up the very first Christmas tree. Queen Victoria lighted the first Christmas tree in the English-speaking world, in 1844 in Windsor Castle. In those days, the lights on Christmas trees were tiny candles. Like other Christmas lights, they symbolized Jesus as the Light of the World.

Gift-giving at Christmas comes from very long ago. Saturn was the important god of agriculture for the Romans, and in his honor they celebrated the Saturnalia, a time of great festivity. They spent seven days in merrymaking and giving gifts.

Christmas cards are tokens of friendship, love and good will. You can see just about all symbols of Christmas on them.

Holly is another loved symbol of Christmas. It is one of our oldest plants. In ancient England, the Druid priests brought holly branches inside in winter, to protect the forest spirits who lived in the holly from bitter cold. The ancient Celts and Teutons in northern Europe gathered holly in December. They reasoned that the gods must favor a plant that can keep its leaves green in the winter. The ancient Romans knew holly, too. They sent sprigs of it to friends during the Saturnalia, as symbols of good will. Christians later came to believe that Christ's crown of thorns must have been made from holly, and that therefore a wreath of holly was a symbol of that crown of thorns.

Santa Claus, of course, is the Christmas symbol everybody knows. The Santa Claus idea began in what is now Turkey, with the legend of a bishop named Nicholas. People believed that he had performed many miracles, especially saving children from harm. Later, he was made a saint. In olden days in Germany, the children knew him as their generous friend who brought them presents and joy. In Holland, his name was Sinter Klaus, and when he finally came to the United States, this was turned into Santa Claus. Perhaps his sleigh and reindeer came from old Scandinavian stories, where the weather god rode around in a little cart pulled by goats.

## Chapter 8

# All Around the World

Here is a very ancient Chinese symbol. It stands for the old Chinese idea that everything in the world seems to be in twos. There are black and white, day and night, fathers and mothers, brothers and sisters, clouds and sunshine, enjoyments and troubles. You'll think of many other sets of twos in your own life.

In this Chinese symbol, the two halves are enclosed by the circle of the world. These two halves are called *Yang* and *Yin*. They stand for the two parts in every person's life. The Chinese say the two parts must work together, like the light of the sky above us and the dark ground we walk on.

Almost everybody has enjoyments and troubles sometimes. And when we have troubles we are

84

glad to have somebody help us. There are a few large organizations who try to help anywhere in the world. These organizations call themselves service clubs. You'll see their symbols in newspapers, on roadsides approaching towns, in hotels and other places where they hold their meetings.

The oldest of these service clubs is Rotary International, whose motto is "Service Above Self." Rotary began in Chicago in the year 1905. It was the idea of a lawyer, Paul Harris, who was new in Chicago, and felt lonely there.

One February evening, Mr. Harris got together with three other strangers in Chicago—a mining engineer, a coal dealer, and a tailor. The four men enjoyed talking about their work, and they decided to meet regularly. Soon they organized a club. They named it *Rotary* because they took turns meeting in each other's offices. It wasn't long before they began to invite other business and professional men to join.

Today, Rotary International has more than 18,000 clubs, with over 800,000 members, in nearly all the countries around the world. Rotary's special community and worldwide service projects include providing student scholarships, and helping foreign students to come to the United States to study.

Look around for other service-club symbols, and you'll surely see those of Lions International and Kiwanis. The Lions Club uses a capital *L* for its symbol. The Kiwanis symbol is a capital *K* inside a circle.

Is there an Elks club in your community? It is the Benevolent and Protective Order of Elks of the United States of America (B.P.O.E.). This is a private fraternal organization (Latin: *frater* = brother), which was founded in New York City in 1868.

Members of a fraternal organization think of each other as brothers, helping and trusting each other as brothers do. The Elks clubs do much charitable work for which they raise large sums of money by selling Christmas trees, holding bingo games in their Elks Temples, and the like.

Your community probably has other fraternities, too. You may know their emblems and

Grand Lodge, Benevolent and Protective Order of Elks of the United States of America.

temples. The Moose, the Eagles, the Knights of Columbus, and the Masons are among the best-known.

Masonic temples show the Masonic emblem over their doors. It is composed of a carpenter's square combined with a compass. With these and other tools, stone masons have always built houses, temples, pyramids and cathedrals. The capital letter G in the center of the emblem is a sign that Masons believe in God. The Masonic order has members in many parts of the world. Its complete name is Free and Accepted Masons; shorter forms are Freemasons, and Masons.

Some ladies wear rings with a colored, five-pointed star. They belong to an organization affiliated with the Masons—the Order of the Eastern Star. The ideals which this star represents are similar to those of the Masons.

Have you ever been in a big airport? If you look out the windows, or go up to the observation deck, you'll see the huge planes with their colorful logos painted on sides and tails.

United Airlines is the largest domestic airline in this country, and has expanded its service to in-

**UNITED**

**JAPAN AIR LINES**

**EASTERN**

clude overseas flights to foreign countries. The United logo is easy to recognize: two U-shapes, one behind the other, with blue on the inside and red on the outside.

At the airport you'll see several logos which make you think of flying birds. One of these, Japan Air Lines, shows a big crane in a circle. In Japan the crane is a symbol of long life. The logo of Eastern Airlines represents a streamlined falcon in flight.

If anybody you know has gone traveling overseas or around the world, you've heard about some of the wonders in foreign lands. One interesting sight in many places is an arch. Arches have different meanings, according to how they are used.

Perhaps the first arch human beings knew was the rainbow. In the Old Testament story of Noah, the rainbow was a symbol of God's promise to mankind, never again to send a flood that would kill everything alive on the earth.

An arch can be a symbol of something coming in and going out. This kind of arch is called a *gateway*. In the United States there is an enormous one in Saint Louis, Missouri—the "Gateway to the West." It is a huge, towering steel structure. A 40-passenger train inside each leg carries you up to the top, 630 feet above the ground, and from there you can see for 30 miles in every direction. The Gateway symbolizes the

spirit of the American pioneers who led the way out to the West.

The emperors in ancient Rome had huge stone arches built, as symbols of their victories in war. The conquered armies and rulers, even kings and queens, would be marched as slaves under the victory arch, to show them that they were of no more value than the horses or cattle used for pulling heavy loads. Some of these old victory arches can still be seen in countries around the Mediterranean Sea. And in Paris you can see the most famous modern victory arch, the *Arc de Triomphe*, which means the Arch of Triumph.

Blaine, Washington, peace arch.

This one was built to be a symbol of the great military victories of Napoleon Bonaparte.

On the border between the United States and Canada stand an arch and a bridge which have become the signs and symbols of peace. At the western end is the Blaine, Washington, peace arch. At the eastern end is the International Peace Bridge which spans the Niagara River and connects Buffalo, New York, and Fort Erie, Ontario. Erected at different times, both commemorate more than a hundred years of peace between the two countries.

International Peace Bridge.

# Index

Castiglione, Italy, 42
Celts, 82
characters, 62
Charles V, 51
Chevrolet, Gaston, 33
Chevrolet, Louis, 33
Chevrolet Motor Division, 33
Chevron company, 37
Chicago, Illinois, 85
China, 16, 18, 63
Chinese, 62, 63, 64, 84
Chinese Buddhist, 64
Chippewa, 55
*chocolatl*, 29
Christian, 17, 82
Christianity, 17, 51
Christmas, 79, 82
Christmas cards, 82
Christmas tree, 81, 86
clocks, 20, 21
Clovis, King of France, 51
coat of arms, 48, 51, 52
color, 69–72, 78
Columbia River, 35
condor, 56–57
Congress, 53
crest, 49
Cross of Lorraine, 43
Cross of St. George, 17
crozier, 19
Crusades, 43

Daily News, The, 35
David, King, 16
de Bouillon, Sir Godfrey, 43
Declaration of Independence, 79
de l'Épée, Abbé Charles Michel, 62
Denmark, 17
Ditrichstein, Prince, 29

Dresden Art Gallery, 29–30
Druid priests, 82
Dunant, Jean Henri, 42
Dürer, Albrecht, 34

Eagles, 87
Easter, 78
Eastern Airlines, 88
Eastman Kodak Company, 32
Edison, Thomas Alva, 23
Egypt, 19, 44, 48
Egyptian, 18, 44, 45, 54
emblem, 42, 44, 53, 73, 86, 87
England, 17, 18, 22, 27, 82
Eostre (Ostara), 78
Ethelwulf, 55
Europe, 15, 21, 29, 49, 52, 54, 59,
    66, 78, 82

figures. *See* numerals
Finland, 17
flag, 13–19, 42, 43, 79
*fleur-de-lis*, 51
Florists' Transworld Delivery (FTD),
    77
Forest City, Iowa, 74
Forest History Society, The, 38
Fort Erie, Ontario, 91
Fourth of July, 79
France, 33, 51, 52
Free and Accepted Masons, 81, 87
Freemasons. *See* Free and Accepted
    Masons
French, 42, 51, 60, 61
French National Institute for Blind
    Youth, 60

gateway, 88–89
General Electric Company, 23

Mediterranean Sea, 90
menorah, 80
Mercury, 77
Mexico, 29, 69
Middle Ages, 22, 49, 52
Middle East, 48
Minnesota Mining & Manufacturing
    Company, 34
Mr. Yuk, 40–41
Mogen David. *See* Star of David
monograms, 34
Moose, 87
Moriarty, Dr. Richard W., 40
music, 66–67

Nabisco. *See* National Biscuit Com-
    pany
National Biscuit Company, 25
National Poison Center, 40
Newington, Connecticut, 36
New World, 79
New York City, 15, 86
New York State, 14, 32, 36
New Zealand, 15
Niagara River, 91
Nicholas, Bishop, 82
Nipper, 27–28
North America, 15, 18, 55, 59
Northern Ireland, 17–18
numerals, 64–66

Ojibwa. *See* Chippewa
Olympic Games, 15
Order of the Eastern Star. *See* Free
    and Accepted Masons
ototeman. *See* totem

Pacific Coast, 56
Palo Alto, California, 36

paramedics, 44
Paris, France, 62, 90
Persia, 78
Perussi, Vincenzo, 47
Phillips 66, 73–74
Phillips, Frank, 73
picture-drawing. *See* characters
Pittsburgh, Pennsylvania, 40
Poland, 53
Pope, the, 19
Portland International Airport, 35–36
Portland, Oregon, 24, 35
prescription, 41
punctuation, 60

Queen of England, 19
Queen Victoria, 81

Ra, 54
RCA Corporation, 27, 28
Red Lion, the, 74
Rochester, New York, 32
Rockies, 57
Roman Empire, 53, 78
Romans, 47, 53, 65, 77, 81, 82
Rome, Italy, 47, 90
Rotary International, 85
Russian, 16, 59

Safeco Insurance Company, 37
Safeway Stores, Inc., 30
St. Andrew's Cross, 17
St. Louis, Missouri, 89
St. Patrick's Cross, 17
Saint Valentine, 78
Santa Claus, 82–83
Saturn, 81
Saturnalia, the, 82
scepter, 19